MW00804776

Signature Solos

8 All-New Piano Solos by Favorite Alfred Composers

Selected and edited by Gayle Kowalchyk

Students love getting new music, and teachers love teaching it! What could be more fun than a book of new solos by several favorite Alfred composers? This collection of piano solos was expressly written for the *Signature Solos* series. A variety of different musical styles is found in each of the books.

As editor of this collection, it was a joy for me to play through many solos to find just the right grouping of pieces for each book. I looked for appealing sounds while considering the technical and musical abilities of students at each level. Students are sure to enjoy playing these "signature solos" for friends and family, informally or on recitals.

Gayle Kowalchyk

Alfred

Alfred Music
P.O. Box 10003
Van Nuys, CA 91410-0003
alfred.com

Copyright © 2015 by Alfred Music
All rights reserved. Printed in USA.

ISBN-10: 1-4706-3214-4
ISBN-13: 978-1-4706-3214-4

Cover Photo
Colored Pencils: © iStock. / Adam Smigielski

Moonlit Waves

Melody Bober

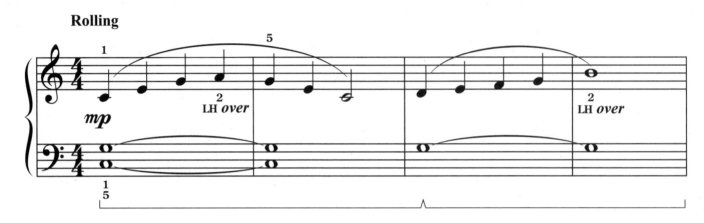

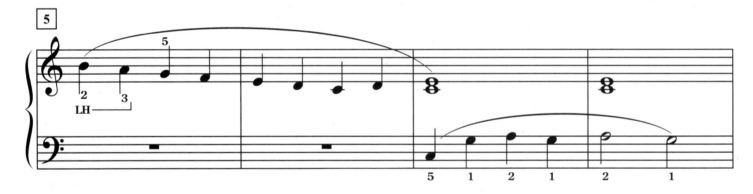

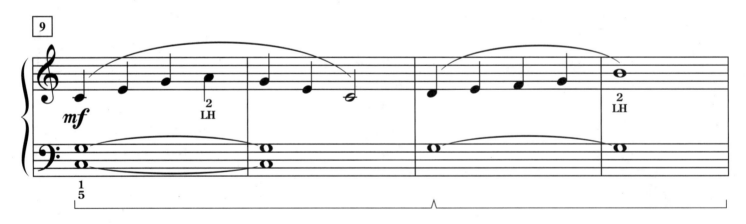

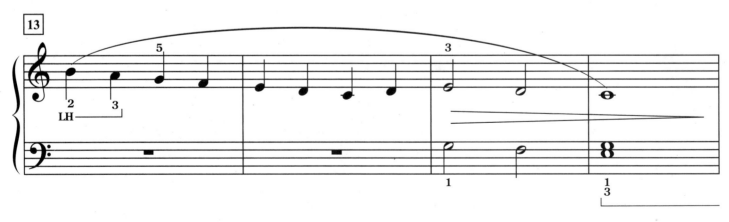

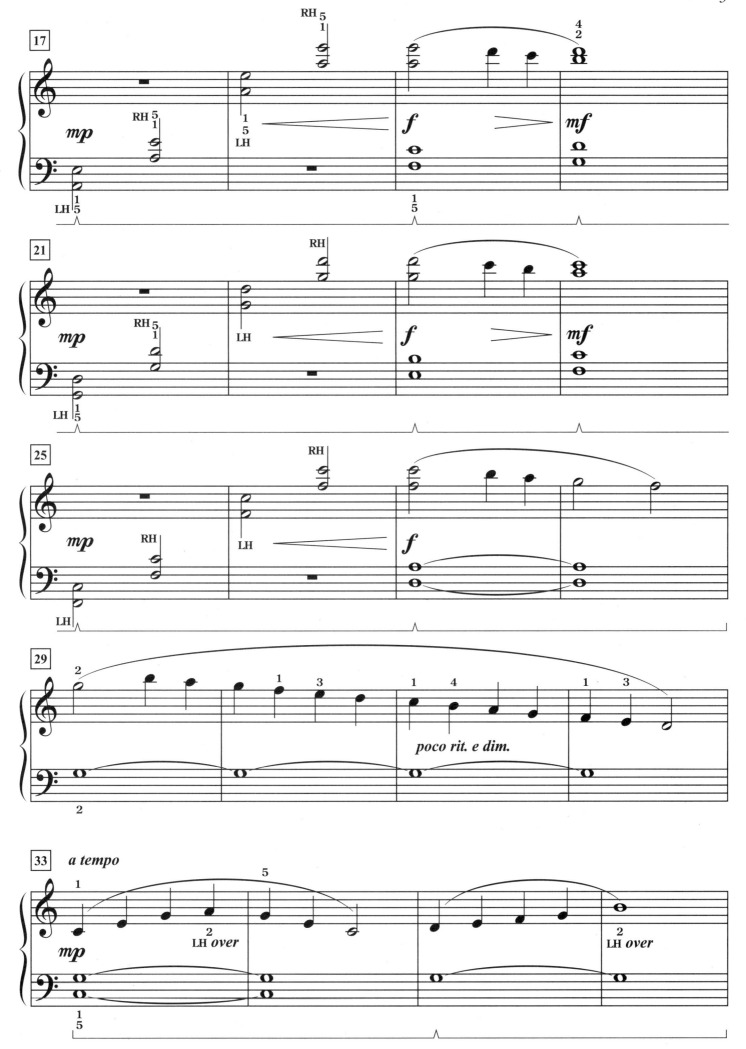

Lights on Broadway

Martha Mier

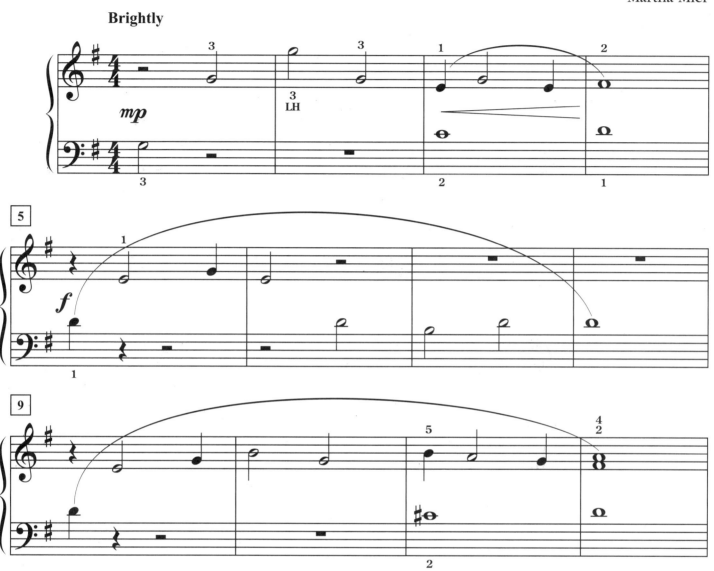

OPTIONAL DUET ACCOMPANIMENT (Student plays one octave higher.)

OPTIONAL DUET ACCOMPANIMENT (Continued)

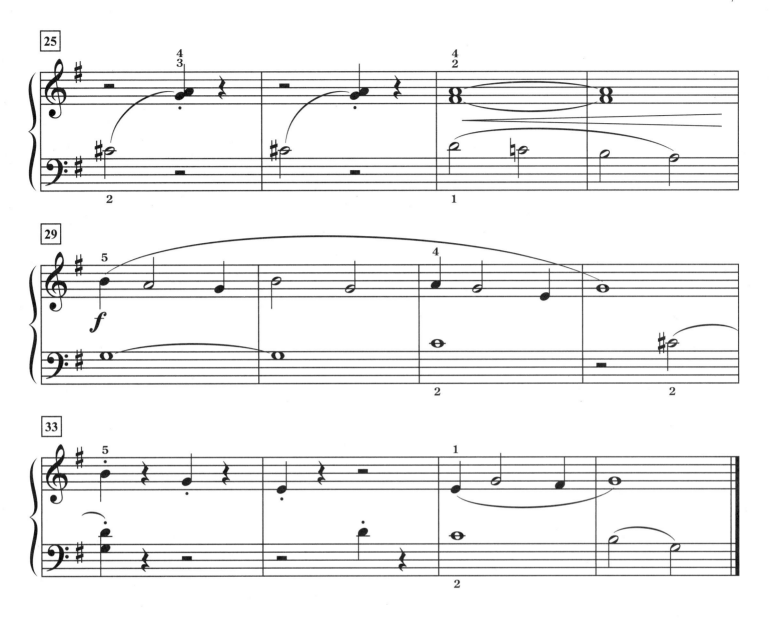

OPTIONAL DUET ACCOMPANIMENT (Continued)

Triad Tarantella

Robert D. Vandall

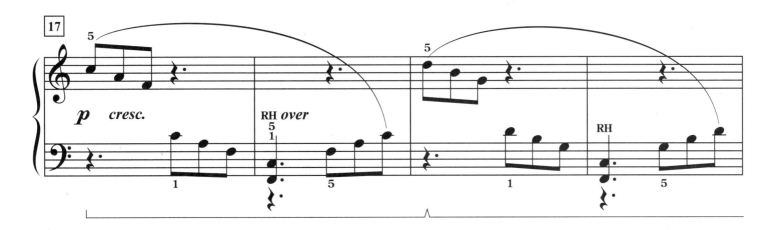

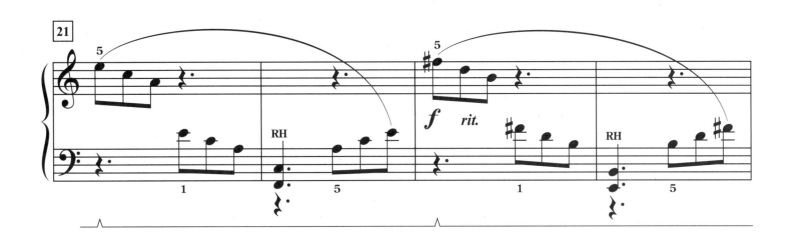

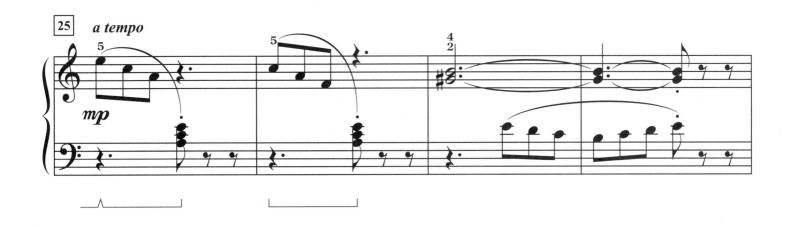

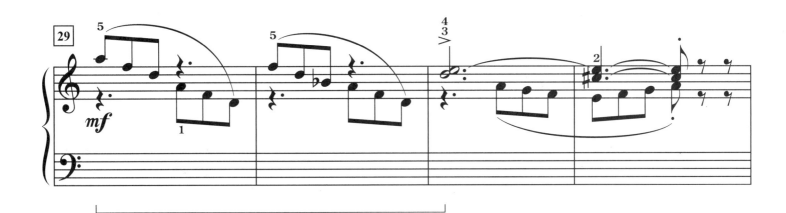

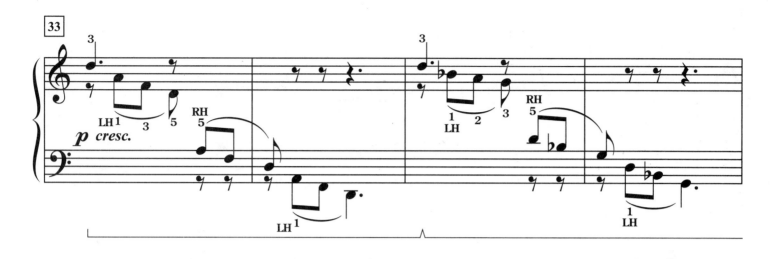

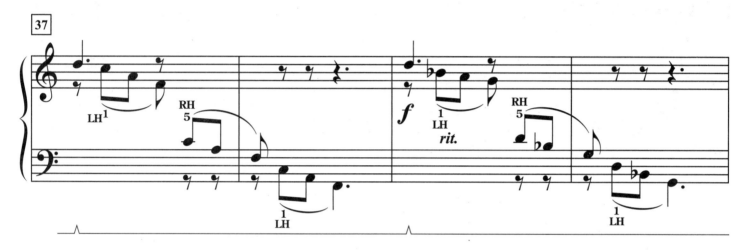

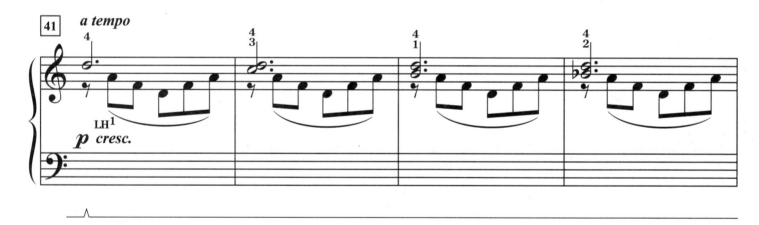

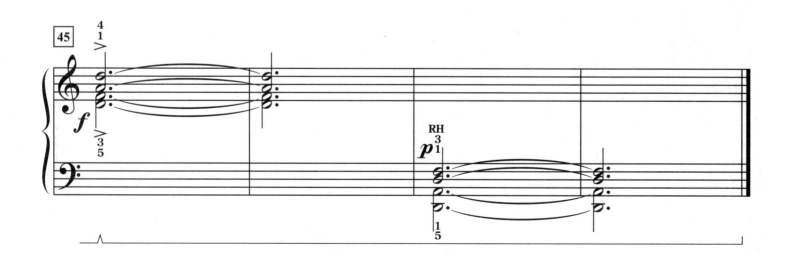

for Shelby, Sophia, and Brennan Johnson

My Dog, Caramel

Bernadine Johnson

Happily

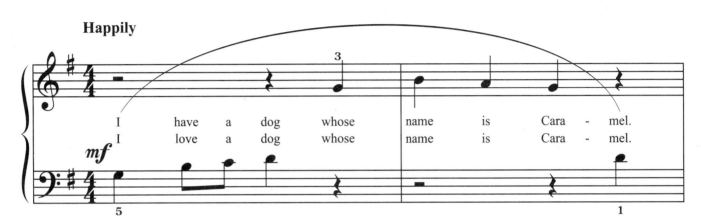

I have a dog whose name is Cara - mel.
I love a dog whose name is Cara - mel.

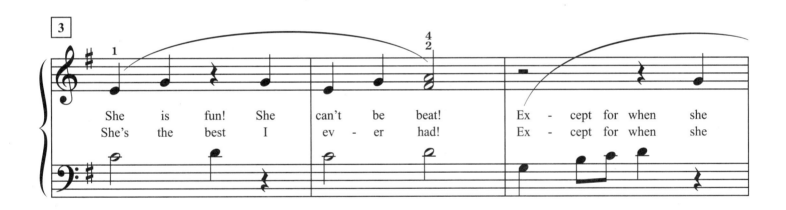

She is fun! She can't be beat! Ex - cept for when she
She's the best I ev - er had! Ex - cept for when she

chewed the shoes I used to wear up - on my feet.
ate the gar - bage, then she was a lit - tle bad.

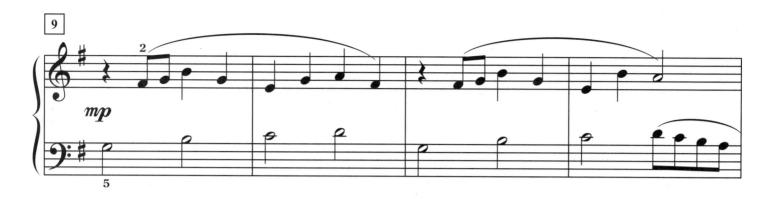

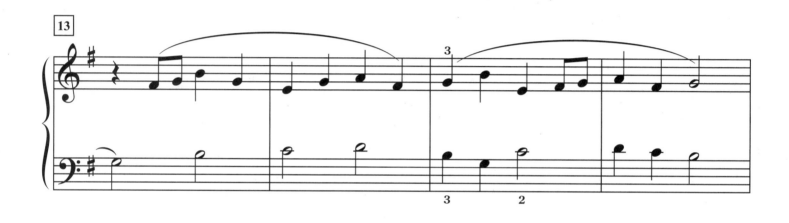

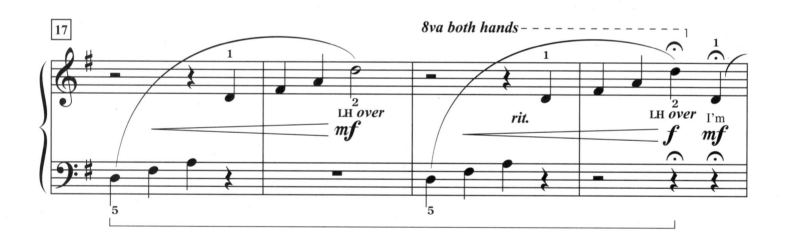

Ex - cept for when she chewed the car - pet, then Mom put her in "time out."

Slowly

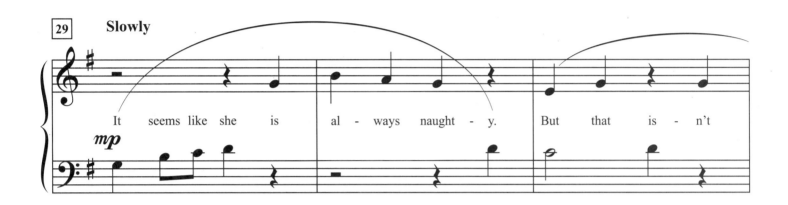

It seems like she is al - ways naught - y. But that is - n't

Happily

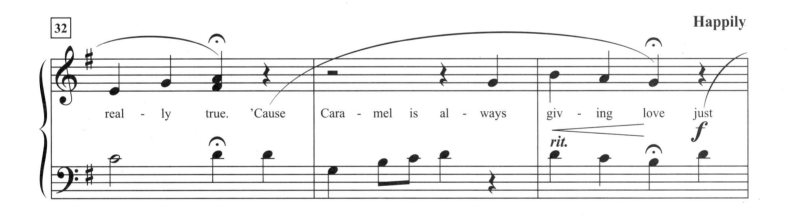

real - ly true. 'Cause Cara - mel is al - ways giv - ing love just

rit.

like a good dog ought to do!

Pogo Stick

Millie Eben

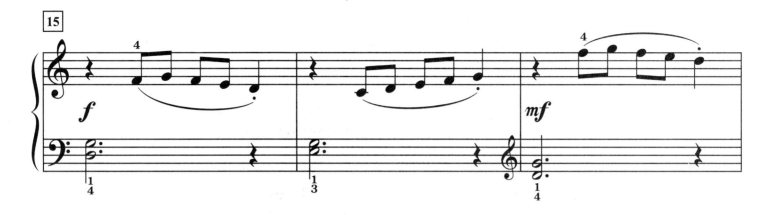

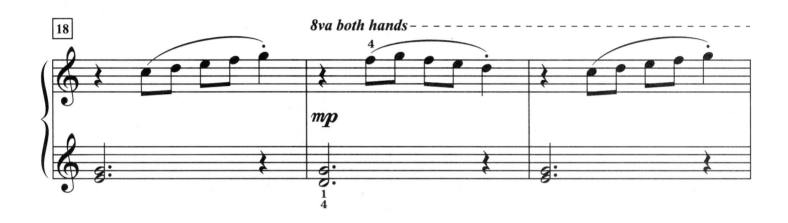

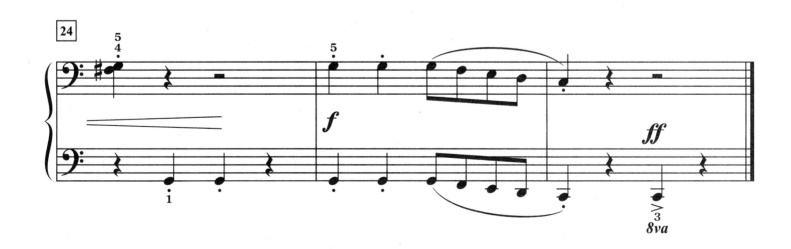

Midnight Storm

Melody Bober

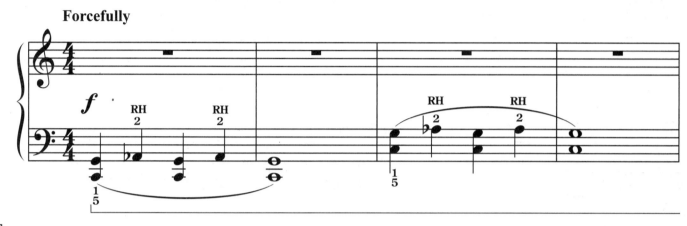

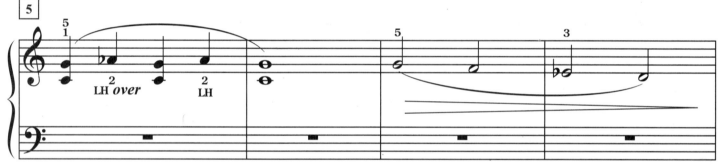

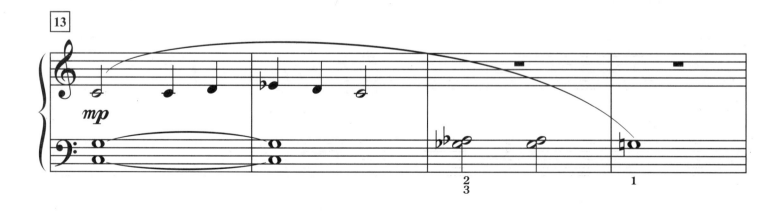

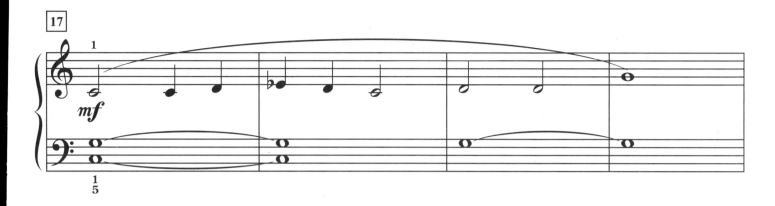

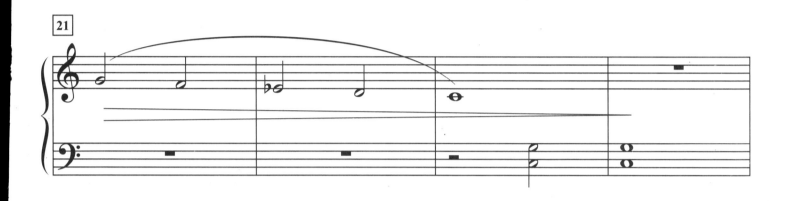

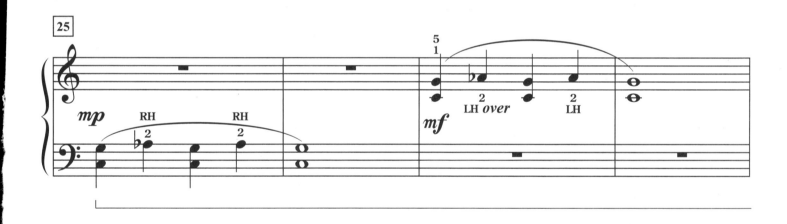

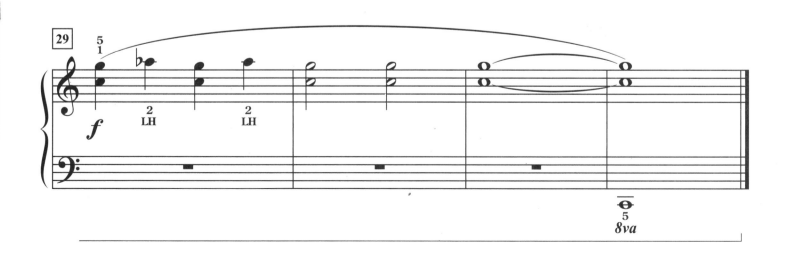

for Timothy Butler

Piano Shark!

W.T. Skye Garcia

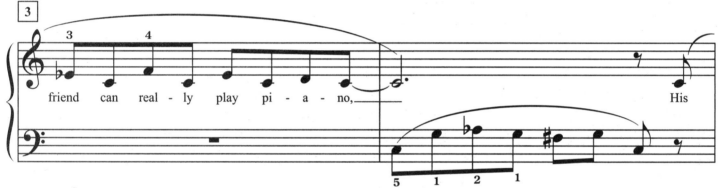

friend can real - ly play pi - a - no,_____ His

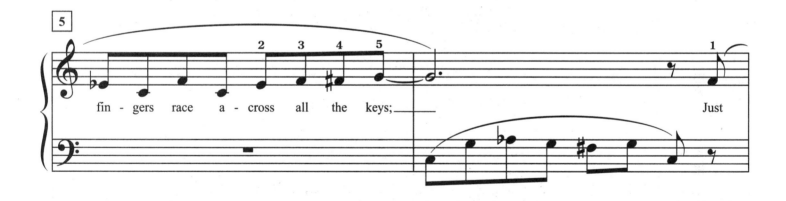

fin - gers race a - cross all the keys;_____ Just

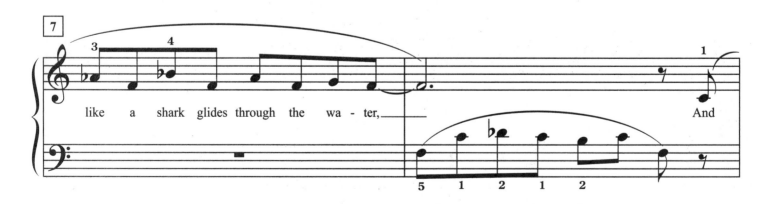

like a shark glides through the wa - ter,_____ And

does it al - most ef - fort - less - ly._____ His

fin - gers dom - i - nate the key - board, just like the shark rules the seas._____

Some -

times he makes the pia - no trem - ble,_____ He

plays the notes so pow - er - ful - ly;_____ It's

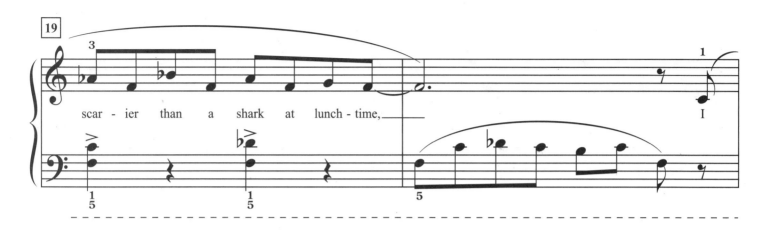

scar - ier than a shark at lunch - time,_____ I

feel the music swal - low - ing me!_____ A

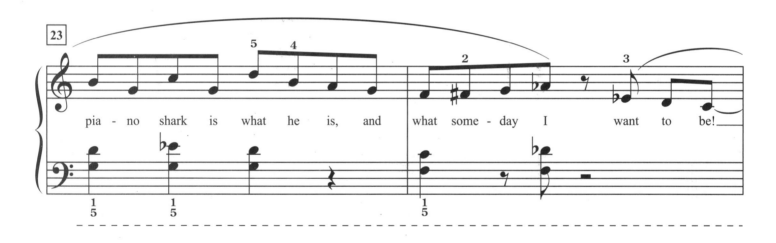

pia - no shark is what he is, and what some - day I want to be!_____

f RH *over*

8va

Swirling Winds

Gayle Kowalchyk
E. L. Lancaster

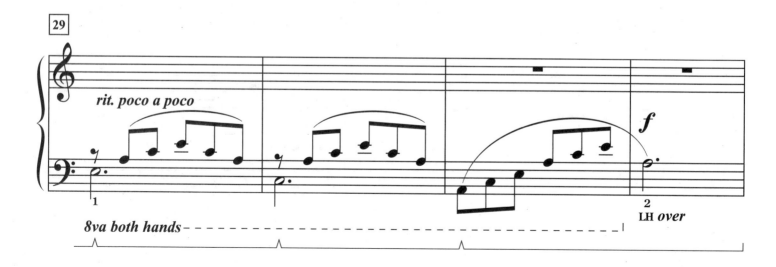